© **2017** Giacomo Giammatteo. All rights reserved. No part of this book may be reproduced or transmitted in any form or by any means, electronic or mechanical, including photocopying, recording, or by any information storage and retrieval system, without written permission from the author, except for the inclusion of brief quotations in a review.

Inferno Publishing Company

Houston, TX

For more information about this book visit my website.

Edition ISBNs

Trade Paperback 978-1-940313-90-0

E-book 978-1-940313-89-4

Cover design by Natasha Brown

Book design by Giacomo Giammatteo

This edition was prepared by Giacomo Giammatteo gg@giacomog.com

❀ Created with Vellum

NO MISTAKES GRAMMAR BITES, VOLUME I

"LIE/LAY/LAID" AND "IT'S/ITS"

GIACOMO GIAMMATTEO

INFERNO PUBLISHING COMPANY

INTRODUCTION

Grammar is important but far too many people seem to want it to be difficult.

Grammar should be easy to learn, at least that's what we believe. With that in mind, I've written several grammar books for adults and several for children. (The No Mistakes Grammar and No Mistakes Grammar for Kids series).

Continuing along the lines of making grammar easy, I've written a new series: No Mistakes Grammar Bites, which will consist of several books, each dealing with two grammar lessons that seem to give people trouble. I'll try to explain them thoroughly but in as much "plain language" as possible. No grammatical terminology unless necessary, and it shouldn't be necessary.

As in all my nonfiction books, the ✓ and ✗ represent correct and incorrect sentences, and the 🕯 means the following sentence is a "tip" to remember.

Each book will sell for an almost-impossible-to-resist ninety-nine cents. Pay ninety-nine cents and learn a lesson for life.

INTRODUCTION

Instead of being the person who wonders whether they've said or written something right, be the one who wonders why someone else didn't say or write it correctly.

LIE, LAY, LAID, AND LAIN

The Easy Way to Use Lie, Lay, and Laid

Let's discuss two of the easier ways to remember how to use the words properly. Since not everyone learns in the same manner, one may suit you better than the other. Either one works, so pick which works best for you.

The Substitution Method

Never again struggle with how to properly use *lie*, *lay*, or *laid*—and even *lain*. With this simple-to-understand chart, you'll immediately see if you're using the words properly.

We'll be using a word-substitution process, and we'll be using commonly known words, so it should be simple. By the way, the lesson includes *lain* but almost nobody uses that word these days, so I don't mention it much.

Look at the chart, then look at the examples that follow.

Tenses of lie/lay	Sit/sat/set	Lie/lay/laid
Present (meaning rest)	Sit	Lie
Past (meaning rest)	Sat	Lay
Present (meaning put down or place)	Set	Lay
Past (meaning put down or place)	Set	Laid
When using 'had' or 'have'	sat	lain
Continuous (meaning rest)	Sitting	Lying
Continuous (meaning put down or place)	Setting	Laying

Now, let's analyze the chart so that you understand it.

If you're confused about which version of *lie* or *lay* to use simply substitute *sit*, *sat*, or *set* to see which sounds right, then refer to the chart, which shows you which word to use.

Let's look at a simple example. If you were going to tell your dog to get down on the floor, would you say "Lie down" or would you say "Lay down"?

Since you're telling your dog to do it *now*, you need to look at the chart next to *lie* and *lay* in the *present* tense. There are only two options—*sit* and *set*.

You wouldn't tell your dog to "set" down, you'd say "sit" down, so looking at the chart, you'd see the answer is *lie*. You would tell your dog to "lie" down.

I could go on for pages, but I think that would only confuse things. If you use the chart, it's easy to determine which word to use by substituting the proper form of *sit* or *set*.

TENSES OF LIE/LAY/LAID AND SIT/SAT/SET

If you were going to write something like "I think I'm going to *lay* down." Before committing to the word *lay*, think of how you'd write the sentence if you were using either of the verbs *sit* or *set*.

If you are "going to *lie/lay* down," it is happening *now*, which means it's present tense. Looking at the chart, we see the only option for "resting" in the present tense is *lie*. So the correct way to write that sentence would be "I think I'm going to *lie* down."

When you want to use any of the verbs *lie, lay, laid, and lain*, think of what you'd say if you were talking about "sitting" or "setting," and use the appropriate word from the chart.

Now we're going to look at a few sample sentences before moving on to the next lesson.

EXAMPLES ARE ALWAYS EASIER

You may need to refer to the chart often when you first start. Afterward, using the words properly should come naturally.

To make it easier, I'll include the chart again (next page or next column, depending on which device you're using to read). I'll also list it further on so you'll have easy access to it.

Tenses of lie/lay	Sit/sat/set	Lie/lay/laid
Present (meaning rest)	Sit	Lie
Past (meaning rest)	Sat	Lay
Present (meaning put down or place)	Set	Lay
Past (meaning put down or place)	Set	Laid
When using 'had' or 'have'	sat	lain
Continuous (meaning rest)	Sitting	Lying
Continuous (meaning put down or place)	Setting	Laying

See if you can get these right without looking at the answers.

- I was tired after working out, so I *laid* down for a nap.
- If you don't feel good, *lay* down for a while.
- The baby just woke. He must have been tired of *laying* down.
- You'd better *lie* down. You don't look so good.
- Shh. The baby's sleeping. My wife just *laid* him down to sleep.
- My wife is sleeping. She just *lay* down to sleep.

NOW LET'S LOOK AT THE ANSWERS.

✗ I was tired after working out so I *laid* down for a nap.

✗ If you don't feel good, *lay* down for a while.

✗ The baby just woke. He must have been tired of *laying* down.

You'd better *lie* down. You don't look so good.

Shh. The baby's sleeping. My wife just *laid* him down to sleep.

My wife is sleeping. She just *lay* down to sleep.

LET's look at why these are right and wrong. In sentence number one, we said:

✗ I was tired after sleeping, so I *laid* down for a nap.

You said "I *was* tired ..." so it happened already, which means it is the *past* tense. When you look at the chart, you see that the only option for resting in the past tense is *lay*. Since that's the case, the sentence would read:

I was tired after sleeping, so I *lay* down for a nap.

Laid is *never* used to mean rest. It is *always* associated with setting or putting something down. Whenever you use laid, you should be able to ask "What" as in "Laid what?"

Two More Examples

I *laid* the flowers on the table. (Laid *what* on the table? The flowers.)

✗ I was tired, so I laid down for a nap. (Laid *what* down for a nap? See, it doesn't work.)

The next few sentences simply show the substitutions.

And I'll include another display of the chart.

Tenses of lie/lay	Sit/sat/set	Lie/lay/laid
Present (meaning rest)	Sit	Lie
Past (meaning rest)	Sat	Lay
Present (meaning put down or place)	Set	Lay
Past (meaning put down or place)	Set	Laid
When using 'had' or 'have'	sat	lain
Continuous (meaning rest)	Sitting	Lying
Continuous (meaning put down or place)	Setting	Laying

✘ If you don't feel good, *lay* down for a while.

This is wrong because you're talking about the present tense—if you don't feel good, rest. Do it *now*. Since it's present tense, you'd use *lie*. What you should say is:

"If you don't feel good *lie* down for a while."

✘ The baby just woke. He must have been tired of *laying* down.

That's wrong because if you look at the chart, the continuous tense meaning to rest would be *lying*. What you should say is:

"The baby just woke. He must have been tired of *laying* down."

You better *lie* down. You don't look so good.

Shh. The baby's sleeping. My wife just *laid* him down to sleep.

Here we use *laid* because your wife physically set/put him down. (As you can see, it answers the "What" question as well. My wife laid what down? She laid the baby down.)

But we're talking about sleep, you might say. We're really not. We're saying my wife *set* something down. That something happens to be the baby. So the baby is *lying* down, but he was just *laid* down.

My wife is sleeping. She just *lay* down to sleep.

This sentence represents the one many people have a problem with. But if you use the chart, you won't go wrong.

Also, you can't get it wrong if you adhere to the rule that *laid* is *never* used to mean sleeping or resting.

SUBSTITUTIONS WORK BEST

Using substitutions is often the easiest way to learn something, especially when trying to learn grammar. So try testing *sit, sat* or *set* as a temporary substitution for *lie, lay,* and *laid,* and I think you'll see it works nicely.

Tenses of lie/lay	Sit/sat/set	Lie/lay/laid
Present (meaning rest)	Sit	Lie
Past (meaning rest)	Sat	Lay
Present (meaning put down or place)	Set	Lay
Past (meaning put down or place)	Set	Laid
When using 'had' or 'have'	sat	lain
Continuous (meaning rest)	Sitting	Lying
Continuous (meaning put down or place)	Setting	Laying

TRIAL EXERCISES

I've include a few more sentences for you below. Choose the right word, then look at the next pages for the correct answers.

1. Where were you? I tried calling, were you (laying/lying) down?
2. What time did you call? I was probably (laying/lying) down.
3. Please be quiet, I just (lay/laid) the baby down.
4. Now I (lay/lie) me down to sleep.
5. Now I (lay/lie) down to sleep.
6. I was tired yesterday afternoon, so I (lie/lay/laid) down for a nap.
7. If you don't feel well, you should (lay/lie) down.
8. Those groceries look heavy. (Lay/lie) them on the table.
9. When it's cold outside, I like to (lay/lie) in bed all day.
10. Bobby said he feels cold. (Lay/lie) him by the fire.
11. Bobby had a fever last night, so my wife (lay/laid) him by the fire.
12. Two hours after she put Bobby down, she felt bad, so she (lay/laid) down herself.

ANSWERS TO TRIAL EXERCISES

1. Where were you? I tried calling, were you *lying* down?

You use *lying* because you would have used *sitting* as a substitute.

2. What time did you call? I was probably *lying* down.

Same reason as above. You'd use *lying* because you would have used *sitting*. As a side note, you don't use *laying* if you're referring to rest, only for setting/putting something down. So it's the same as *laid* in that regard. Add that rule to your book. You don't use *laying* to refer to rest—ever.

3. Please be quiet, I just *laid* the baby down.

You'd use *laid* because you *set* something down—the baby.

4. Now I *lay* me down to sleep.

So, yes, as illogical as it sounds, this age-old saying is grammatically correct because it is talking about "laying" something down. The fact that it's talking about laying yourself down, which would not be easy to do, makes no difference from a grammatical standpoint.

It would be no different than saying "Now I lay the elephant down to sleep." We know you couldn't pick up an elephant and set it down, just as we know you couldn't pick up yourself and set yourself down, but from a grammatical standpoint, it's logical.

5. Now I *lie* down to sleep.

This one is different because you're not setting anything down, so it would be *lie*. In the previous example, we said "Now I *lay me* down to sleep."

6. I was tired yesterday afternoon, so I *lay* down for a nap.

You're talking about rest, and you're referring to the past (yesterday), so according to the chart, you'd use *lay*.

7. If you don't feel *good*, you should *lie* down.

Again, look at the chart. It's speaking of resting, and it's present tense, so it's *lie*.

This was a double trick. Notice I changed the "feel well" to "feel good." We'll cover that in another section.

8. Those groceries look heavy. *Lay* them on the table.

This is the opposite of the two previous sentences. You're not speaking of rest, and it's present tense, so it's *lay*.

9. When it's cold outside, I like to *lie* in bed all day.

Try the substitutions for this one. "When it's cold outside, I like to (sat/set) in bed all day." As you can tell, they don't work, which means it's *sit*, and according to the chart, that means you should use *lie*.

10. Bobby said he feels cold. *Lay* him by the fire.

This one is similar to the children's prayer. You're laying something down—Bobby—so you would use *lay*.

11. Bobby had a fever last night, so my wife *laid* him by the fire.

This follows the same logic as the previous sentence. Since your wife is "laying" something down and not resting herself, the proper word is *laid*. Remember, if you run into trouble, use the chart. It clears things up immediately.

12. Two hours after she put Bobby down, she felt bad, so she *lay* down herself.

This one is different. She is no longer "laying" something down, she is resting. Looking at the chart, we see that since it concerns resting, and since it's past tense, the proper word would be *lay*.

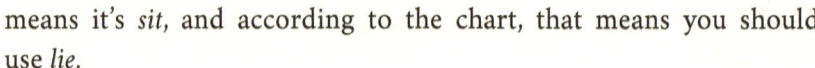 **Remember, you don't use "laying" if you're talking about rest, and you don't use *laid* if you're talking about rest.**

If you can keep that in mind, you may be able to remember this: If you're talking about *rest*, you can only use the following:

- lie=present tense.
- lay=past tense.
- lying=any continuous use (present, past, or future) (I am lying. I was lying. I will be lying.)

I hope you now have a good grasp on when and where to use *lie*, *lay*, *laid*, or *lain*.

LESSON TWO

I don't want to leave you with the impression that all you just read in part one was worthless, so consider it a great back-up. But if you learn the three rules below, you won't need the back-up. If you forget the rules, you have the *substitutions* to fall back on.

As far as I'm concerned, this covers things quickly and efficiently. Learn the following rules, and you should be set.

🞿 The first rule is a simple reminder. *Never* use "laid" or "laying" to mean rest or sleep. If you remember that, all you need to work on are the words "lie" and "lay."

🞿 If you have a temptation to use the word "laid" associated with rest or sleep, use "lay" instead.

🞿 And if you are tempted to use "laying" associated with rest, use "lying."

The rules that follow are easy, and there are only three of them. Learn them, and you've mastered the use of lie/lay/laid/lain.

THE RULES

1. If you start to say, "I was *laying* down when you called," realize that "laying" *cannot* be used with rest so use "lying" instead. "I was *lying* down when you called."
2. If you start to say, "I *laid* down," realize that "laid" *cannot* be used with rest so use "lay" instead. "I got tired last night and *lay* down."
3. Any time that you use "lie" or "lay" meaning to *rest*, check the tense in your head. If you're talking about *now*, the word to use is "lie." If you're talking about something that already happened, use "lay."

That's it. You're done. You now are a master regarding the use of "lie, lay, laid, and lain."

IT'S AND ITS

This seems like a simple thing to dedicate so much time to, but the fact is that many (and I mean many) confuse the usage. When I did a search on Google for the difference between "it's" and "its," I got 311 *million* results.

With so many people wanting to know the difference, I feel we should address it. The difference between the usage is fairly simple; you just have to be aware of it.

One Is Possessive. One Is a Contraction

Its indicates possession and does not require an apostrophe. The following sentence is an example:

- The company and *its* employees will have a picnic this weekend.

We don't use an apostrophe in that sentence because the word denotes ownership, so to speak, and *its*, when it denotes ownership, does not take an apostrophe. Another example of that is *hers*. We would say:

- She owns the car. It's *hers*. We wouldn't say "It's her's."

The most confusion over *it's* and *its* seems to occur when the possessive is involved. People have a tendency to include an apostrophe when ownership is involved.

- I know that dog; *it's* Bob's. He also owns Slick's mother.

As you can see in the example, usage can sometimes be confusing. We've mixed using *it's* as a contraction with two possessives (Bob's and Slick's). Some people have a tendency to make *it's* a possessive also, but, in this case, it's not functioning as a possessive; it's simply a contraction for "it is."

There's an Easy Way to Tell Which Form to Use

And when I say easy, I mean *easy*.

The only time you use an apostrophe with *it's* is when it represents two words—"it is" or "it has." Examples follow.

- *It's* raining. (It is raining.)
- *It's* been raining all week. (It has been raining all week.)
- *It's* been a long time since we've seen each other. (It has been a long time since we've seen each other.)

If you ever question which form to use, try substituting "it is" or "it has," and see if it works. If it doesn't, you don't need an apostrophe. If it does, use one. More examples follow:

- The picnic will be at the company's park. *It's* their land.
- It is their land.
- *It's* a crime how much interest banks charge.
- It is a crime how much interest banks charge.
- You see that dog? *It's* Bear's puppy. Bear is *its* father.

You see that dog? It is Bear's puppy. Bear is its father.

The last one was a little more confusing because we mixed a contraction with a possessive. But when you try to substitute "it is" for the second use, it doesn't work. Try it.

Bear is it is father.

See? It doesn't work. The bottom line is that no matter who you are or what you do, when it comes to finding the right form of *its* or *it's*, *it's* (it is) only a matter of checking it with a simple substitution. It would be great if all grammar problems were so easy.

Here are two more examples so you can try it yourself.

- *It's* a crime what they charge for prescriptions.
- The dog and *its* father were both biters.

Now try substituting "it is" or "it has" in each sentence, and see how it works.

It is a crime what they charge for prescriptions.

The substitution works, so the right answer is *it's*.

The dog and it is father both were biters.

The substitution doesn't work, so the right answer is *its*, without an apostrophe.

If you use substitution to verify, you should never go wrong again.

ACKNOWLEDGMENTS

I want to thank my wife and my four grandkids. They give me the inspiration to keep going.

I also need to mention the wonderful beta readers, who helped me so much with this book. Without them it would have likely been a jumbled mess.

Rose Hutchison

Tom Thayyil Thomas

Emiliana Giammatteo

Craig Thompson

Paul Campbell

ABOUT THE AUTHOR

Giacomo Giammatteo is the author of gritty crime dramas about murder, mystery, and family. He also writes non-fiction books including the No Mistakes Careers series, No Mistakes Publishing, No Mistakes Grammar, and No Mistakes Writing.

When Giacomo isn't writing, he's helping his wife take care of the animals on their sanctuary. At last count they had forty-five animals—eleven dogs, a horse, six cats, and twenty-six pigs.

Oh, and one crazy—and very large—wild boar, who takes walks with Giacomo every day and happens to also be his best buddy.

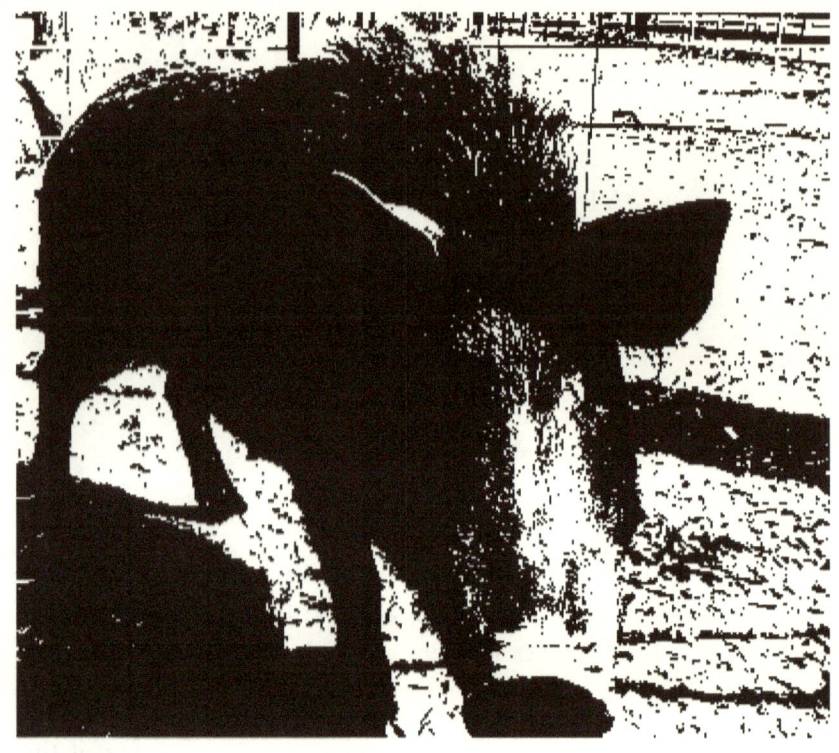

nomistakespublishing.com
gg@giacomog.com

ALSO BY GIACOMO GIAMMATTEO

You can see all of my books here.
And you can buy them on the platform of your choice.

This brings up a thought: with more than fifty books out now, it is becoming difficult to try to update the list in the back of all of them. If you want to know what books I have out, use the link above, which takes you to my website, or download the latest copy of my GG recommended reading list, which is free.

Nonfiction :

Careers:

No Mistakes Resumes, Book I of No Mistakes Careers

No Mistakes Interviews, Book II of No Mistakes Careers

Grammar:

Misused Words, No Mistakes Grammar, Volume I

Misused Words for Business, No Mistakes Grammar, Volume II

More Misused Words, No Mistakes Grammar, Volume III

Visual Grammar (this is a compilation of volumes I–III with a bit of new information added. It also includes pictures. The world's first visual grammar book)

Misused Words and Then Some, No Mistakes Grammar, Volume V

More Grammar:

No Mistakes Grammar Bites, Volume I, Lie, Lay, Laid, and It's and Its

No Mistakes Grammar Bites, Volume II, Good and Well, and Then and Than

No Mistakes Grammar Bites, Volume III, That, Which, and Who, and There Is and There Are

No Mistakes Grammar Bites, Volume IV, Affect and Effect, and Accept and Except

No Mistakes Grammar Bites, Volume V, You're and Your, and They're, There, and Their

No Mistakes Grammar Bites, Volume VI, Passed and Past, and Into, In To and In

No Mistakes Grammar Bites, Volume VII, Farther and Further, and Onto, On, and On To

No Mistakes Grammar Bites, Volume VIII, Anxious and Eager, and Different From and Different Than

No Mistakes Grammar Bites, Volume IX, A While and Awhile, and Envy and Jealousy

No Mistakes Grammar Bites, Volume X, Could've and Should've, and Irony and Coincidence

Writing:

No Mistakes Writing, Volume I—Writing Shortcuts

No Mistakes Writing, Volume II—How to Write a Bestseller

No Mistakes Writing, Volume III—Editing Made Easy

Publishing:

How to Publish an eBook, No Mistakes Publishing, Volume I

How to Format an eBook, No Mistakes Publishing, Volume II

eBook Distribution, No Mistakes Publishing, Volume III

Print on Demand—Who to Use to Print Your Books, No Mistakes Publishing, Volume IV

Other nonfiction

Uneducated

Whiskers and Bear—Volume I, Sanctuary Tales *A Collection of Animal Stories, Volume II*, Sanctuary Tales

More Animal Stories, Volume III, Sanctuary Tales *Surviving a Stroke—or Two*

Life and Then Some

Fiction:

Friendship & Honor Series:

Murder Takes Time

Murder Has Consequences

Murder Takes Patience

Murder Is Invisible

Murder Is a Promise

Blood Flows South Series:

A Bullet For Carlos: A Connie Gianelli Mystery

Finding Family, a Novella

A Bullet From Dominic

The Good Book

Redemption Series:

Necessary Decisions: A Gino Cataldi Mystery

Old Wounds

Promises Kept, the Story of Number Two

Premeditated

Rules of Vengeance Series: (Fantasy)

Light of Lights (the beginning, a novella)

A Promise of Vengeance

Undeniable Vengeance

Consummate Vengeance

Note. The Light of Lights is a novella. It's about 100 pages long and sets the stage for the series. The other books in the series are about 800 pages long.

OTHER BOOKS

You can always see the current and coming-soon books on my website.

Fiction:

***Memories for Sale* (mystery/sf)**

***The Joshua Citadel* (SF novella)**

Children's Books:

No Mistakes Grammar for Kids, Volume I—Much and Many

No Mistakes Grammar for Kids, Volume II—Lie and Lay

No Mistakes Grammar for Kids, Volume III—Bring and Take

No Mistakes Grammar for Kids, Volume IV, "Would've, Should've" and "Your and You're"

No Mistakes Grammar for Kids,Volume V, "There, They're, and Their" and "To, Too, and Two"

Shinobi Goes to School—Life on the Farm for Kids, Volume I

Fiona Gets Caught, Life on the Farm for Kids, Volume II

Coco Gets a Donut, Life on the Farm for Kids, Volume III

Squeak Gets a Home, Life on the Farm for Kids, Volume IV

Biscotti Saves Punch, Life on the Farm for Kids, Volume V

Coming Soon:

The Adventures of Adalina, Volume I, Adalina and the Five Tiny Bears

The Adventures of Adalina, Volume II, Adalina and the Underwater Bears

Get on the mailing list and you'll be sure to be notified of release dates and sales.

[Mailing list](#)

And don't forget to leave a review!

www.ingramcontent.com/pod-product-compliance
Lightning Source LLC
Chambersburg PA
CBHW021200080526
44588CB00008B/438